Preschool Skills

Table of Contents

ISBN 978-1-60418-262-0

How to Use This Book

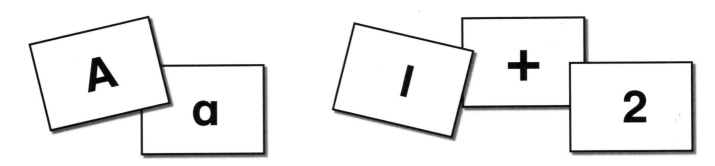

This book was developed to help children master basic skills that form the foundation for children's learning. The stronger their foundation is in the basics, the easier children will be able to progress through more challenging tasks.

All children learn at their own rate; therefore, introduce concepts to children when developmentally appropriate. In addition, provide opportunities for hands-on learning to reinforce the skills covered within the activity pages.

The following activities are provided to use as follow-up ideas or enrichment activities to supplement the ones in this book.

- Tracing is a wonderful way for children to work on fine-motor skills. Dot-to-dot books provide an excellent opportunity for children to work on fine-motor as well as sequencing skills. Another way to work on tracing skills is with salt or sand. Use the lid of a shoe box and cut a few pieces of paper to fit inside the box top. Using a thick black marker, draw a variety of wavy, straight, and curvy lines. Cover the paper with a thick layer of salt or sand. Encourage children to trace the lines through the salt or sand.

- Cutting activities also help children develop and improve fine-motor skills. Draw shapes and lines with a thick marker for children to cut out. Begin with simple lines and angles, such as an *L* or half of a square. When they have mastered a right angle, practice with curves. Next, try basic shapes, such as a square, circle, oval, and triangle. Introduce different materials for children to cut, such as fabric, paper bags, aluminum foil, and paper plates, as they show progress with cutting.

 CD-104312 • © Carson-Dellosa

How to Use This Book

At the back of this book are removable flash cards to use for basic skill practice and enrichment activities. Pull the flash cards out and cut them apart.

The following are just a few ideas for how to use these flash cards. It is recommended that you begin each activity using only a few cards. Gradually introduce cards as children become more proficient. It is also suggested that you repeat these activities with children.

- Encourage children to put the 26 uppercase letter flash cards in alphabetical order. Use the lowercase alphabet flash cards to see if children can match each with its corresponding uppercase letter. Discuss objects that begin with the letter. Brainstorm other objects that begin with the same sound.

- Place both sets of numeral flash cards in separate stacks. Have children put the numeral flash cards in order from 0 to 10 and count the numbers. Then, take the number word flash cards and help them match the number word with the numeral. Once this has been mastered, try playing concentration by matching the number word to the numeral.

- Put out the numeral flash cards in order. Using beans or counters, encourage children to put the correct number of beans in front of each number card. Discuss which groups of objects have more and less.

- Show children the colorful shape flash cards one at a time and discuss each. For example, talk about the square flash card. Have children find the square objects in the room around them. Ask them what other shapes look like the square. Discuss the characteristics of a square, such as its four sides.

Name _____

Following a Maze

Follow the maze to help each hen get to her eggs.

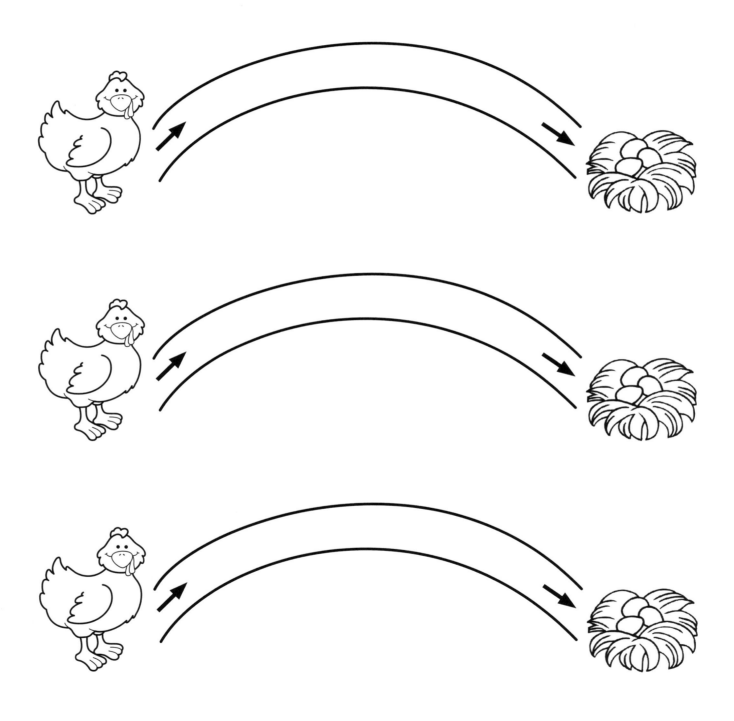

Following a Maze

Follow the maze to help each rabbit get to its carrot.

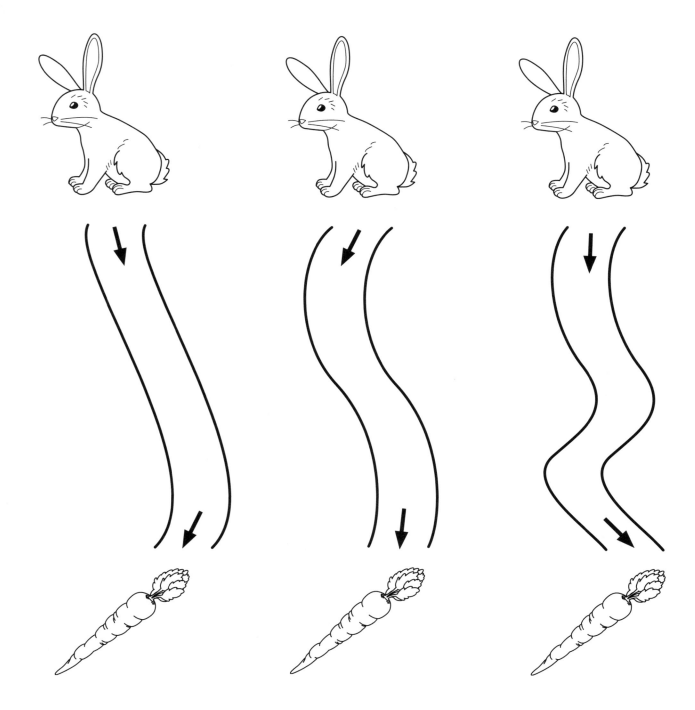

Name _____

Following a Maze

Follow the maze to help each farmer get to his cow.

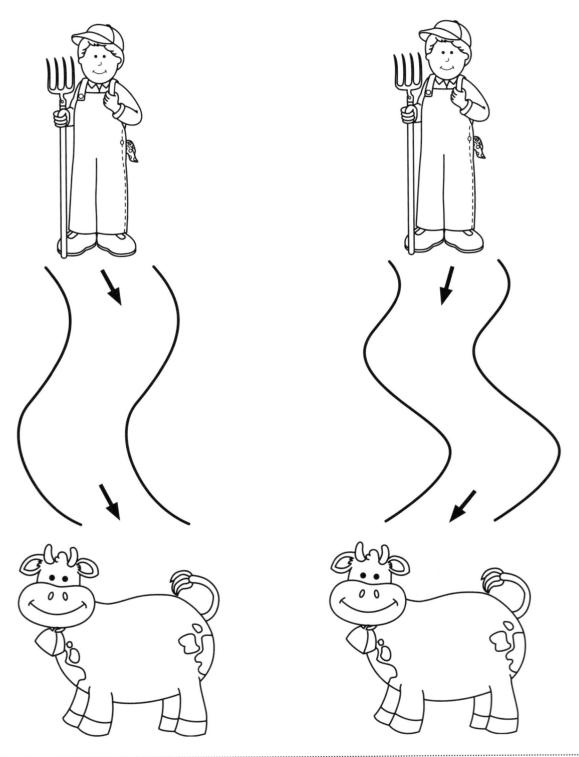

Name _____

Following a Maze

Follow the maze to help the car get to the finish line.

Name _____

Following a Maze

. . . .

Follow the maze to help the ant get to his leaf.

   CD-104312 • © Carson-Dellosa

Tracing Straight Lines

Trace the path that the rain takes to get to each garden.

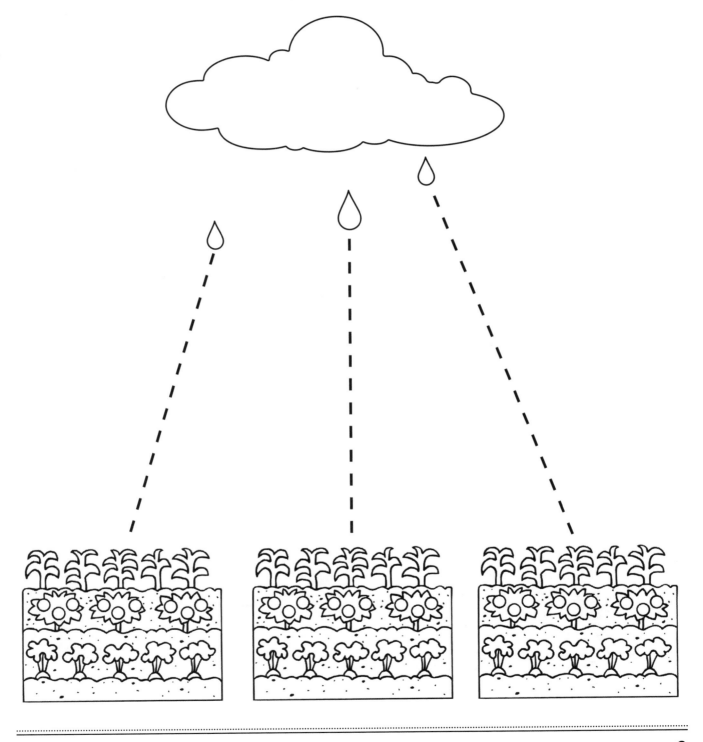

Tracing Straight Lines

Trace the path that each bird takes to get to its nest.

Tracing Lines

Trace the dotted lines to help the fish swim.

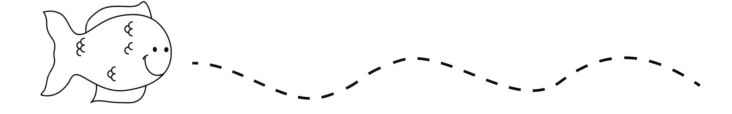

Name _____

Tracing Curved Lines

Trace the dotted lines to help each bee find its flowers.

Name _____

Tracing Curved Lines

Trace the dotted lines to help each rocket fly to the moon.

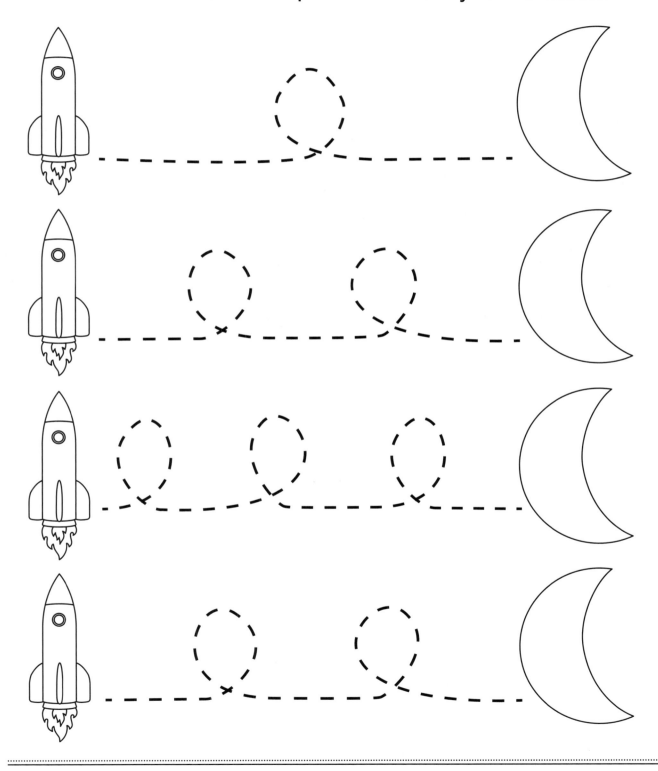

Tracing Curved Lines

Trace the dotted lines to complete the pizza dough. Color the pizzas.

Name _____

Tracing Triangles

Trace the dotted lines to complete the **triangles**. Color each triangle a different color.

Name _____

Tracing Squares

Trace the dotted lines to complete the **squares**. Color the squares.

CD-104312 • © Carson-Dellosa

Tracing Rectangles

Trace the dotted lines to complete the **rectangles**. Color the rectangles.

Name _____

Tracing Circles

Trace the dotted lines to complete the **circles**. Color the circles.

Tracing Hearts

Trace the dotted lines to complete the **hearts**. Color the hearts.

Name _____

Tracing Rhombuses

Trace the dotted lines to complete the **rhombuses**. Color the rhombuses.

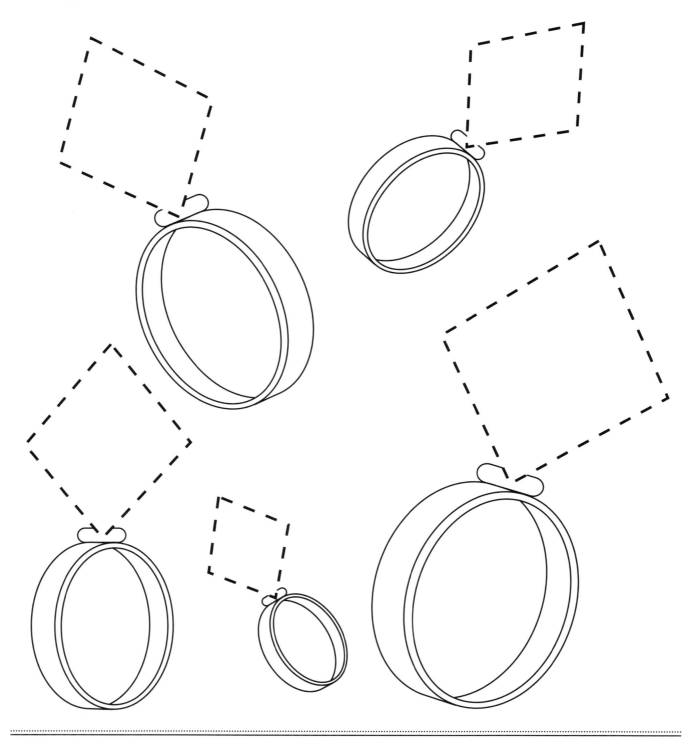

CD-104312 • © Carson-Dellosa

Tracing Stars

Trace the dotted lines to complete the **stars**. Color the stars.

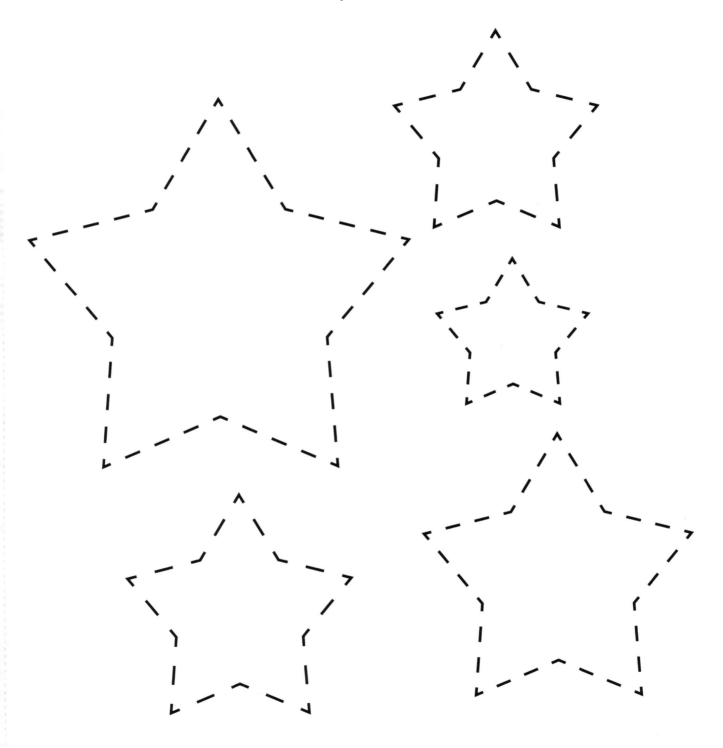

Tracing Shapes

Trace the dotted lines to complete the picture. Color the picture.

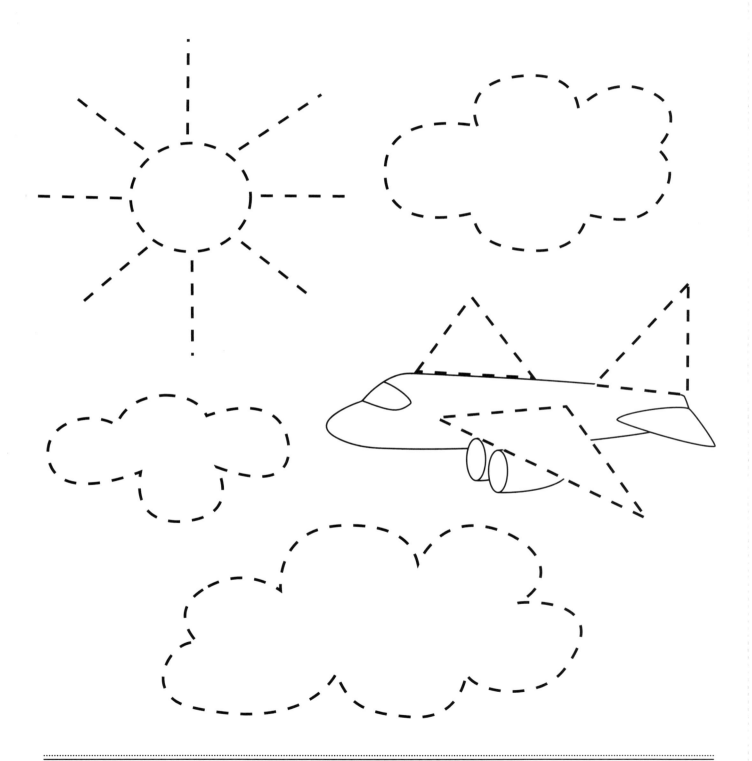

 CD-104312 • © Carson-Dellosa

Tracing Fish

Trace the dotted lines to complete the **fish**. Color the fish.

Name _____

Cutting Straight Lines

Cut the paths the swimmers take.

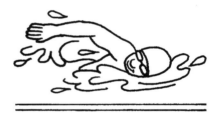

Name _____

Cutting Straight Lines

Cut the path the bus takes to get to school.

Cutting Curved Lines

Cut the trails made by the airplane.

Cutting Curved Lines

Cut the path each skier takes to get to the bottom of the hill.

Name _____

Cutting Stars

Color the **stars** yellow. Cut out the stars.

CD-104312 • © Carson-Dellosa

Cutting Hearts

Color the **hearts** red. Cut out the hearts.

Name _____

Cutting Bubbles

Color the **bubbles** your favorite color. Cut out the bubbles.

Cutting Leaves

Color the **leaves** green. Cut out the leaves.

Name _____

Cutting Raindrops

Color the **raindrops** light blue. Cut out the raindrops.

Cutting Hourglasses

Color the **hourglasses** different colors. Cut out the hourglasses.

Cutting Kites

Color the **kites** your favorite color. Cut out the kites.

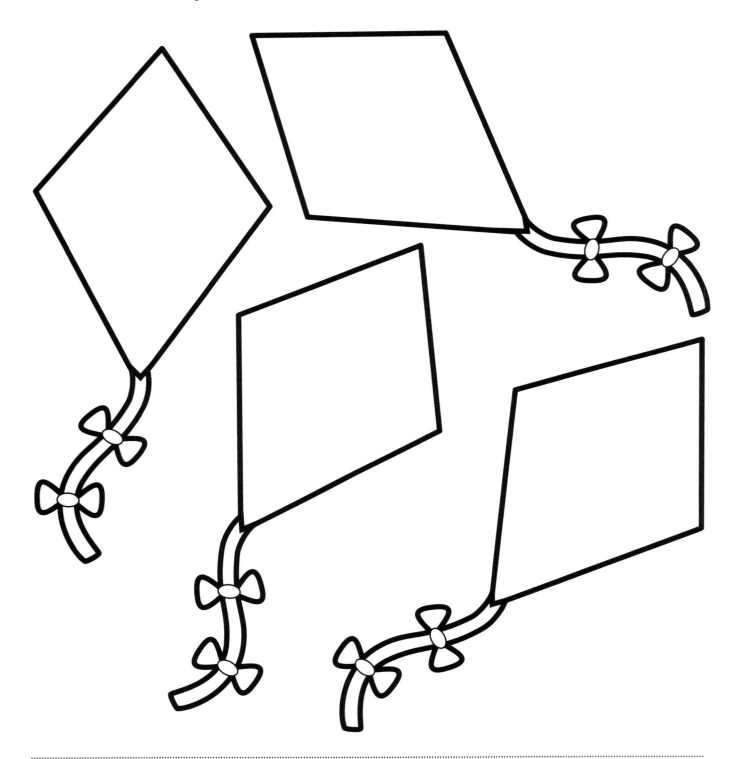

Name _____

Completing Objects

Make the **second** shape look like the **first** shape in each box.

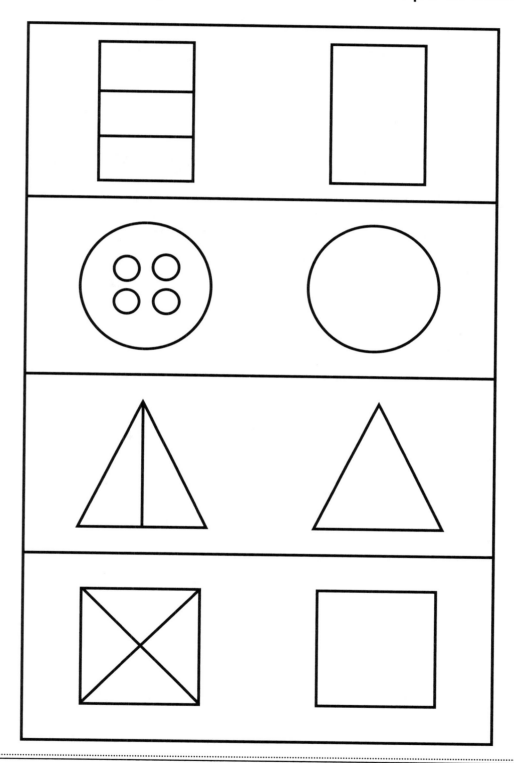

Name _____

Completing Objects

Make the **second** shape look like the **first** shape in each box.

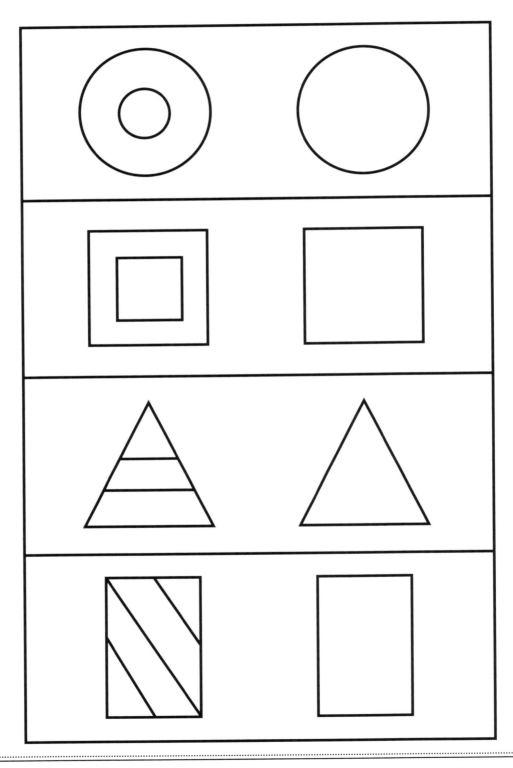

CD-104312 • © Carson-Dellosa

Name _____

Completing Objects

Make the **second** shape look like the **first** shape.

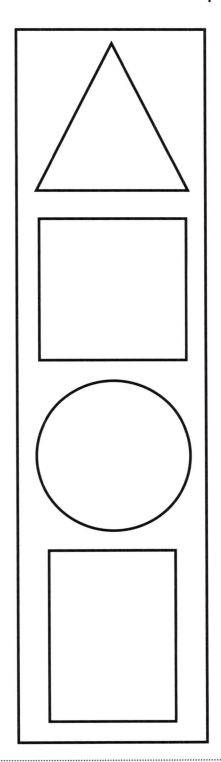

Name _____

Completing Objects

Make the **second** shape look like the **first** shape.

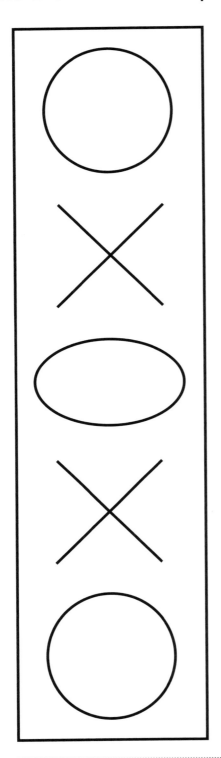

CD-104312 • © Carson-Dellosa

Name _____

Completing Objects

Color the **second** shape to look like the **first** shape in each box.

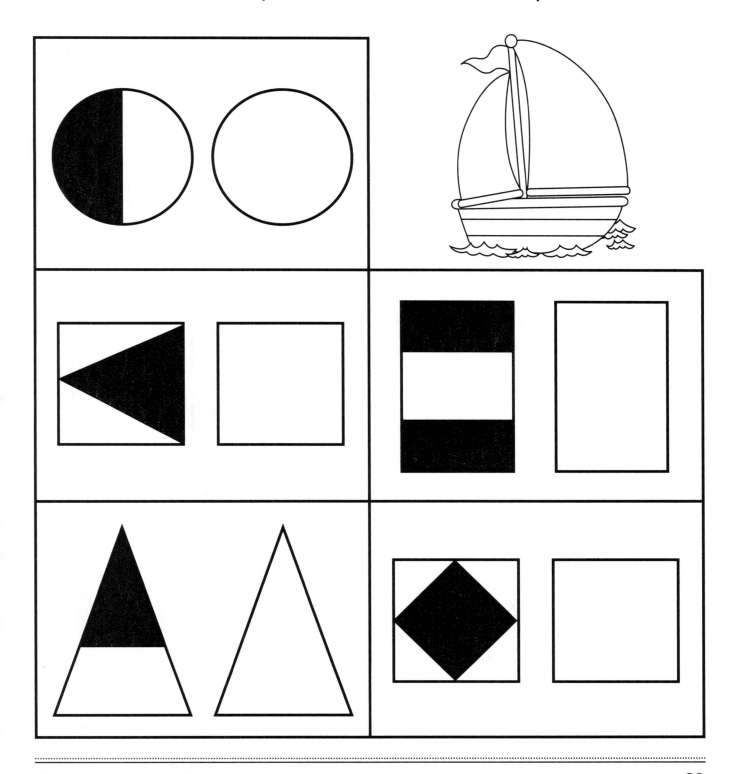

Completing Objects

Color the **second** shape to look like the **first** shape in each box.

Name _____

Completing Objects

Make the **right** half of the butterfly look like the **left** half. Color the picture.

Completing Objects

Make the **left** half of the house look like the **right** half.
Color the picture.

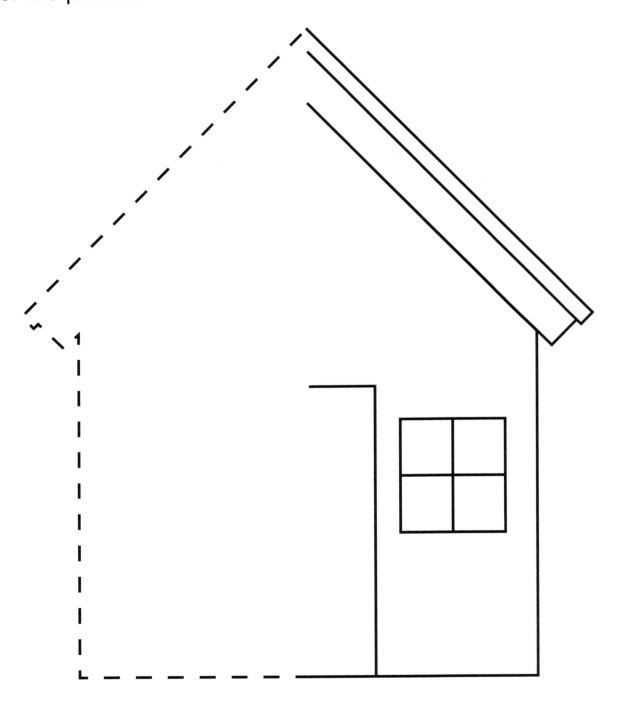

Completing an Object

Make the **right** half of the star look like the **left** half.
Color the picture.

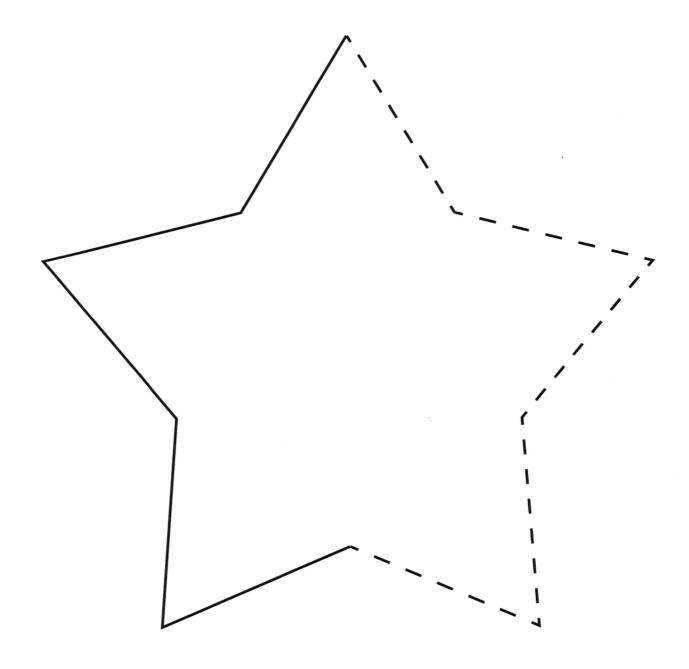

Name _____

Drawing an Object

Follow the steps to draw your own snail.

 CD-104312 • © Carson-Dellosa

Name _____

Drawing an Object

Follow the steps to draw your own dragonfly.

Name _____

Drawing an Object

Follow the steps to draw your own fish.

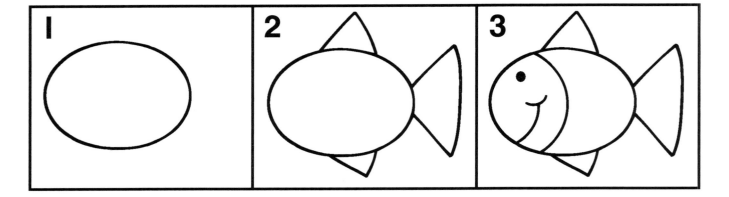

Name _____

Comparing Size

Color all of the **big** cats orange. Color all of the **small** cats gray.

Name _____

Comparing Size

Color all of the **big** bells yellow. Draw a circle around all of the **small** bells.

CD-104312 • © Carson-Dellosa

Comparing Size

Color the **largest** object in each group.

 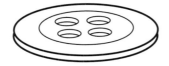  

Comparing Size

Color the **largest** object in each group.

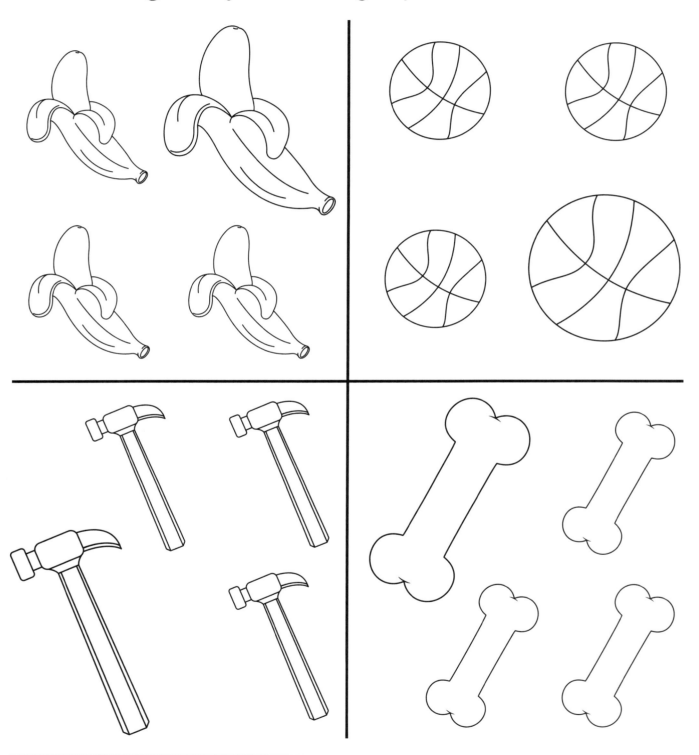

Name _____

Comparing Size

Color the **smallest** object in each group.

Name _____

Comparing Size

Color the **smallest** object in each group.

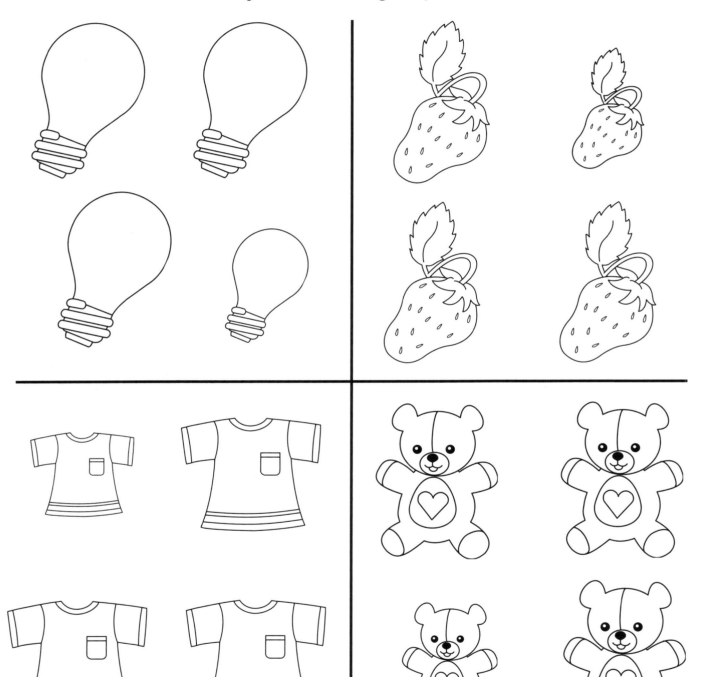

 CD-104312 • © Carson-Dellosa

Comparing Length

Color the **shortest** object in each group.

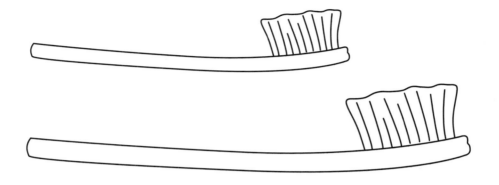

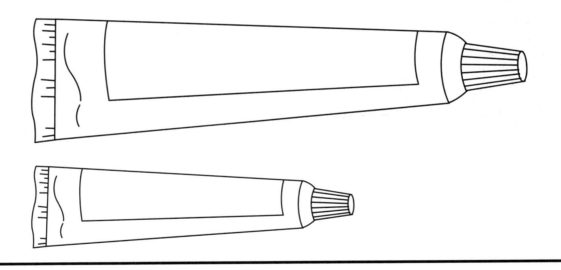

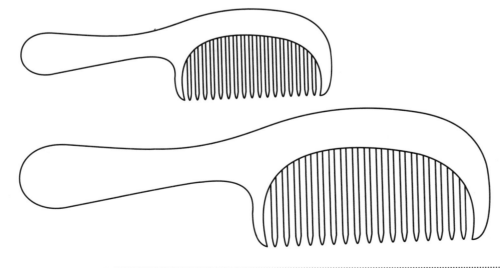

Name _____

Comparing Length

Color the **longest** object in each group.

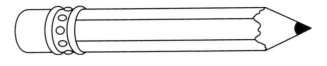

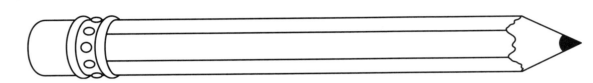

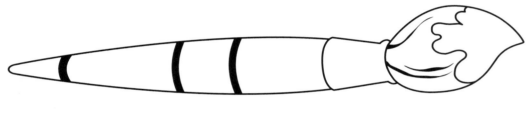

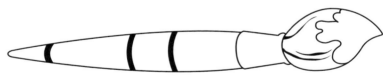

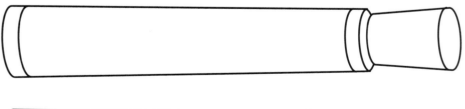

  CD-104312 • © Carson-Dellosa

Comparing Length

Color the **long** snakes yellow. Color the **short** snakes brown.

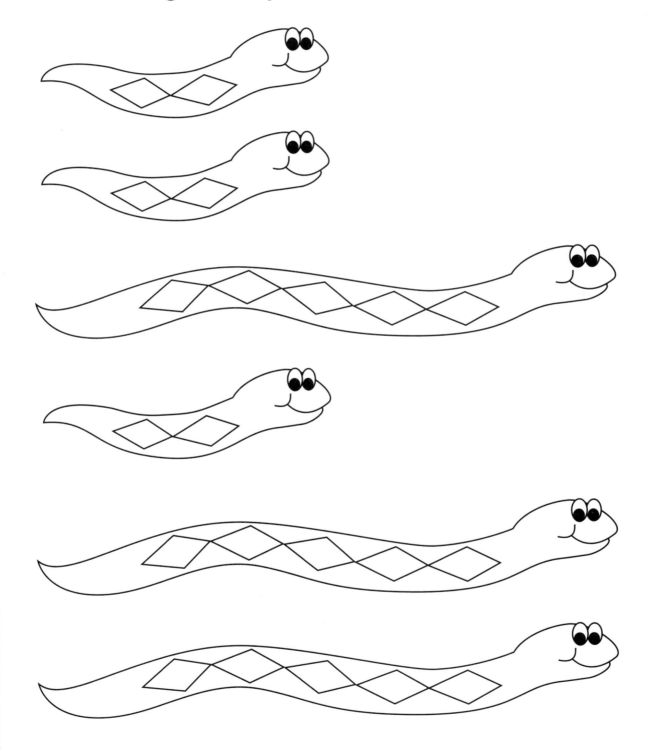

Comparing Length

Color the **tall** trees green. Color the **short** trees brown.

Comparing Amount

Circle the group of objects that has **less** in each row.

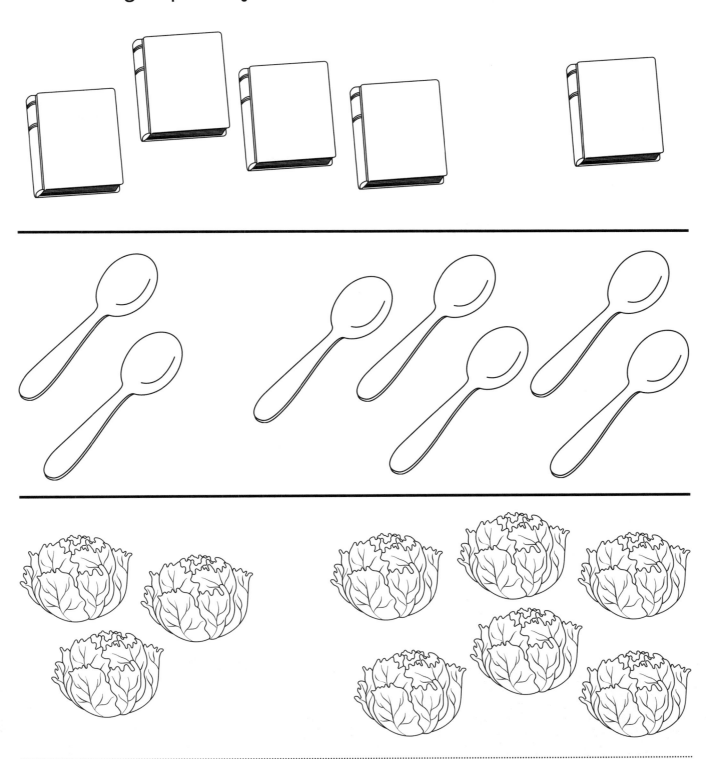

Comparing Amount

Circle the group of objects that has **more** in each row.

 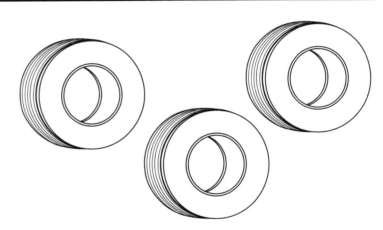

 CD-104312 • © Carson-Dellosa

Recognizing Same and Different

Draw lines to match the socks that are the **same**.

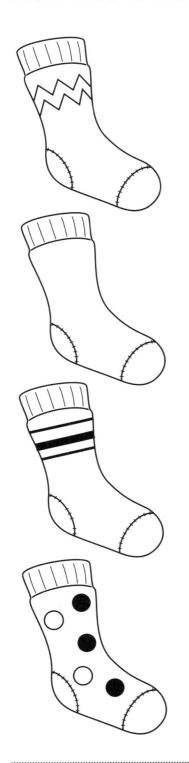

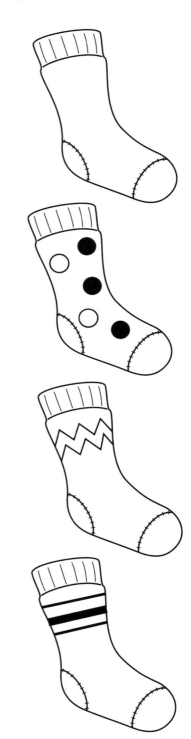

Name _____

Recognizing Same and Different

Color the two shapes that are the **same** in each group.

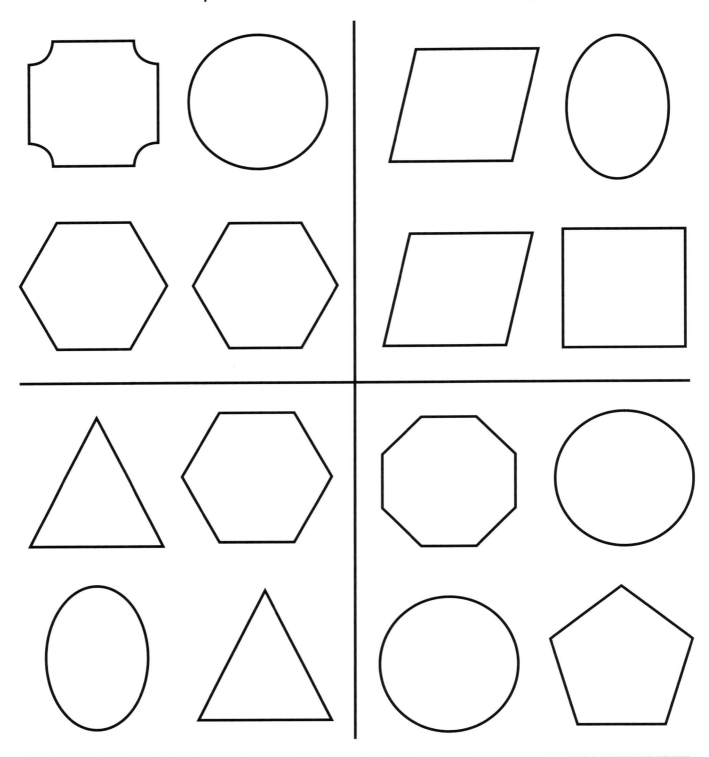

Name _____

Recognizing Same and Different

Color the two shapes that are the **same** in each group.

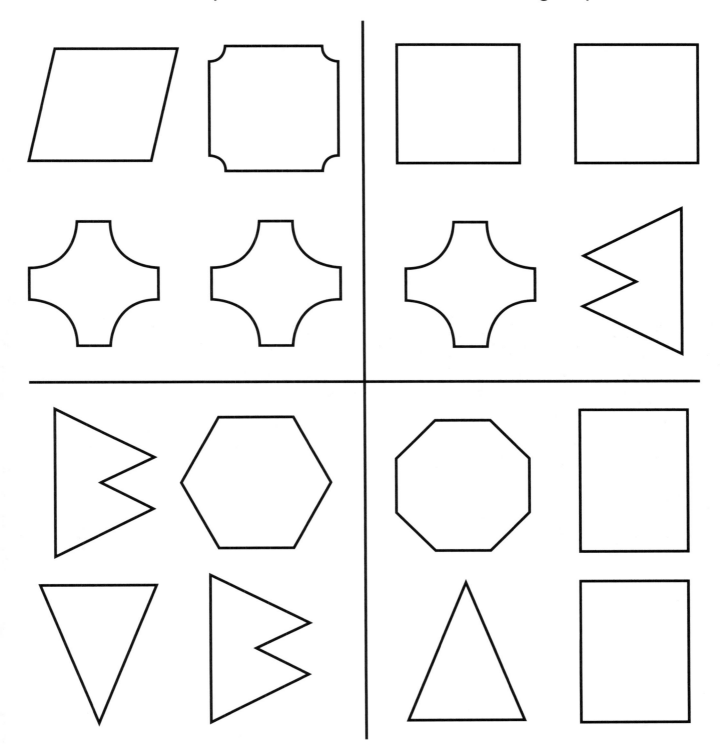

Recognizing Same and Different

Circle the two objects that are the **same** in each group.

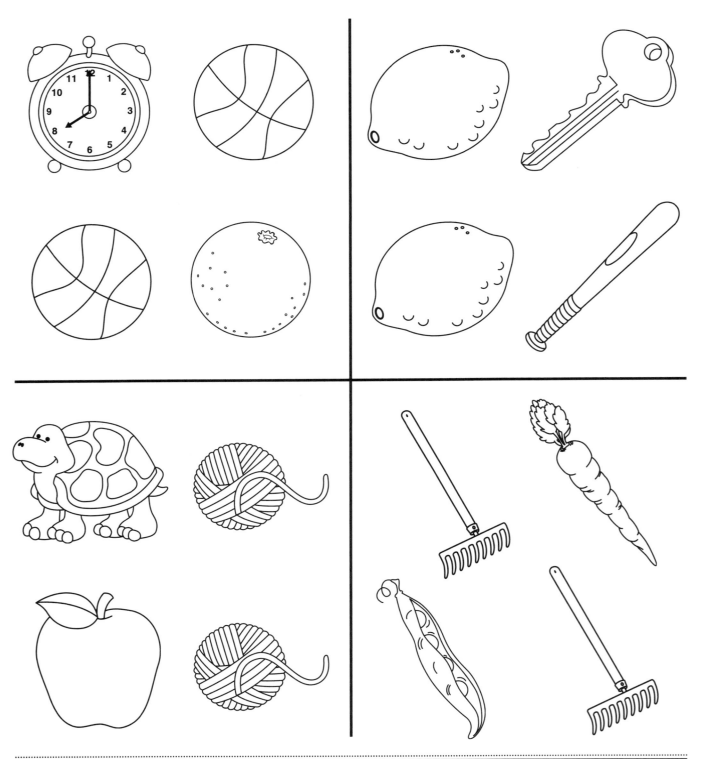

CD-104312 • © Carson-Dellosa

Name _____

Recognizing Same and Different

Color the object that is **different** from the others in each group.

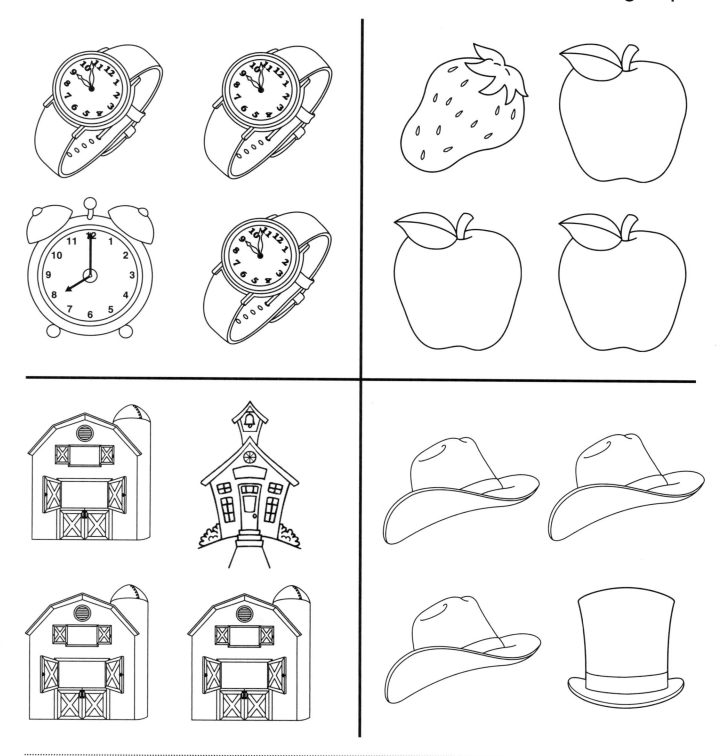

Recognizing Same and Different

Color the eggs that are the **same** as the egg in the box.

Recognizing Same and Different

Color the ladybugs that are **different** from the ladybug in the box.

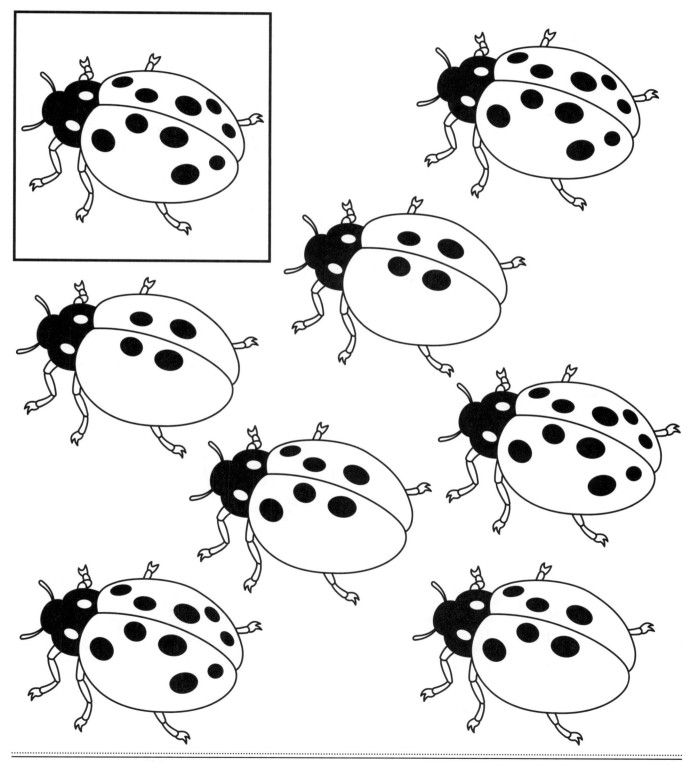

Name _____

Recognizing Same and Different

Color the shape that is **different** from the others in each row.

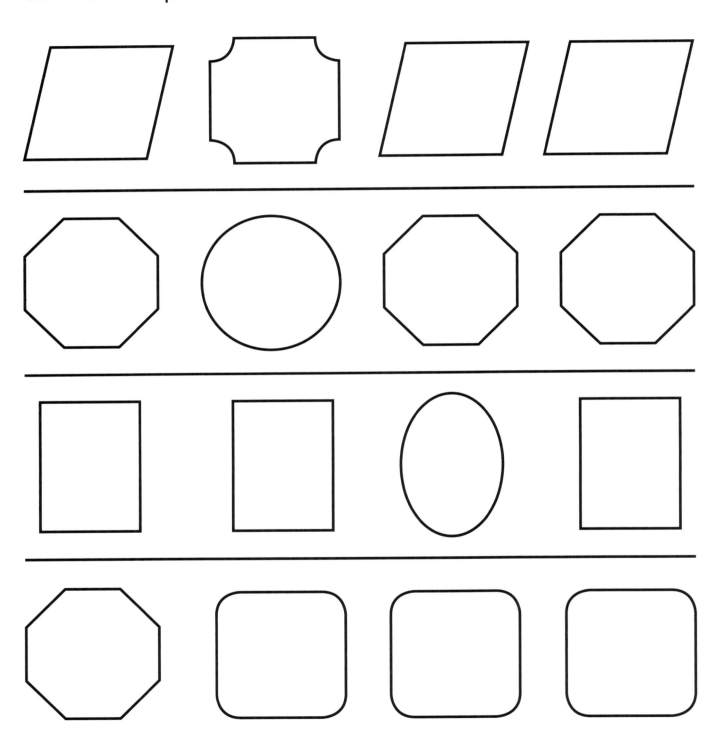

CD-104312 • © Carson-Dellosa

Name _____

Recognizing Same and Different

Color the shape that is **different** from the others in each row.

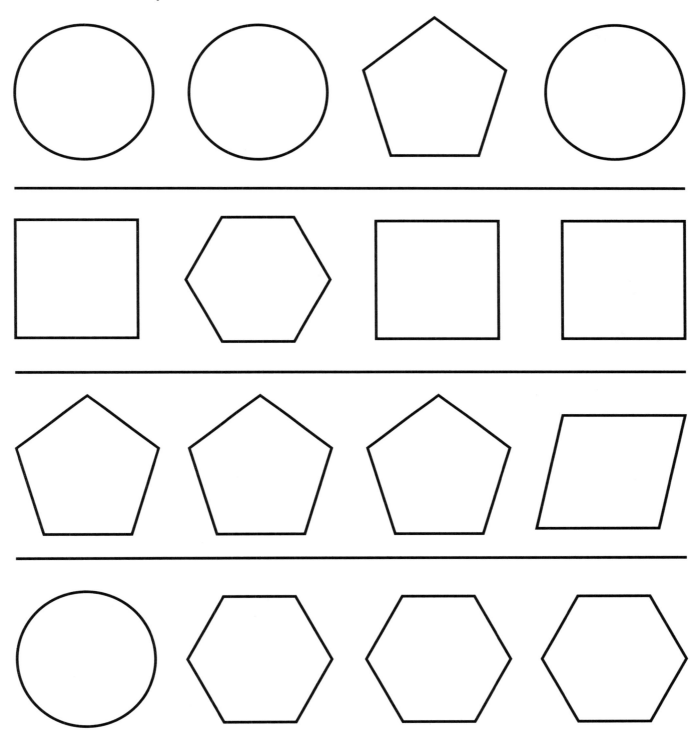

Recognizing Same and Different

Color the object that is **different** from the others in each row.

 CD-104312 • © Carson-Dellosa

Name _____

Recognizing Same and Different

Color the birds that are the **same** as the bird on top.

Name _____

Recognizing Same and Different

Color the dice that are **different** from the one on top.

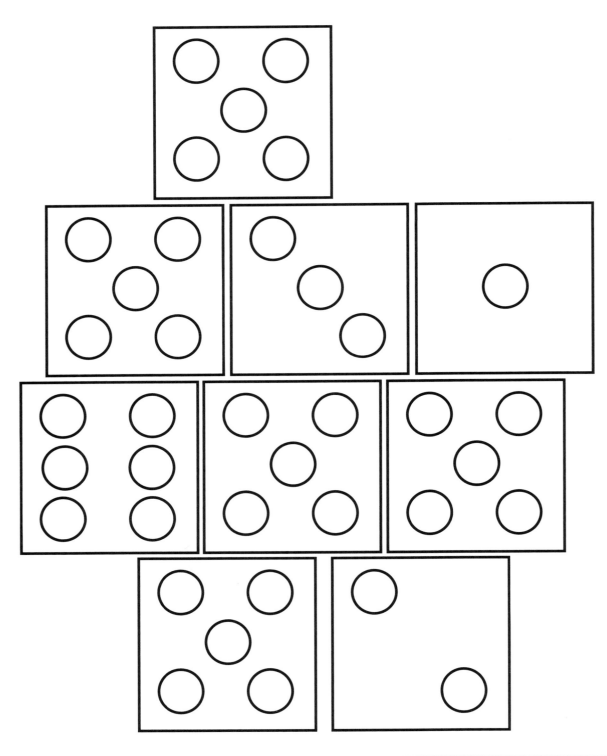

 CD-104312 • © Carson-Dellosa

Name _____

Identifying Circles and Squares

Color the **squares** green. Color the **circles** yellow.

Identifying Ovals and Rectangles

Color the **ovals** brown. Color the **rectangles** red.

Identifying Rhombuses and Triangles

Color the **triangles** purple. Color the **rhombuses** pink.

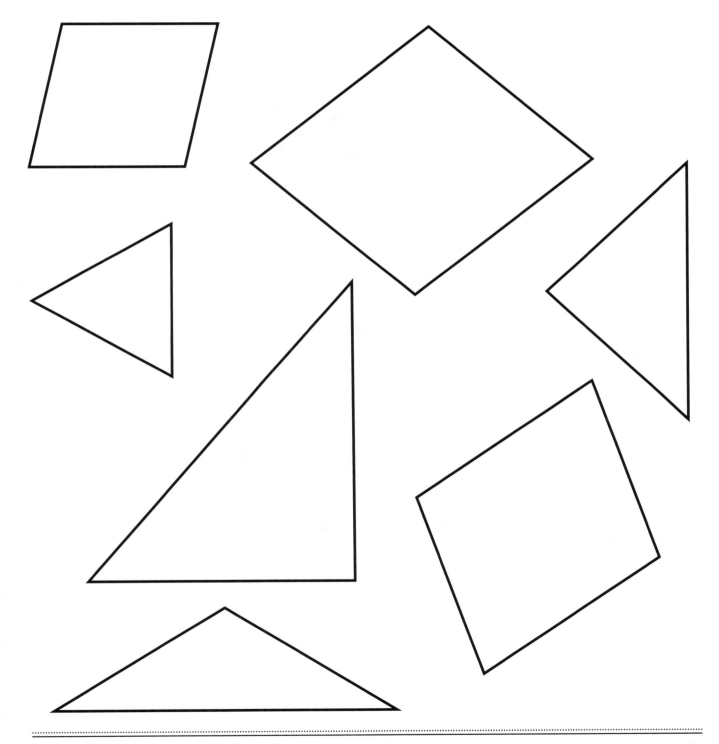

Identifying Circles

Find and color 4 **circles**.

 CD-104312 • © Carson-Dellosa

Identifying Circles

Find and color 5 **circles**.

Identifying Squares

Find and color 5 **squares**.

Identifying Squares

Find and color 5 **squares**.

Identifying Rectangles

Find and color 5 **rectangles**.

Name _____

Identifying Triangles

Color the **triangles** blue.

Identifying Circles

Color the **circles** green.

Name _____

Identifying Squares

Color the **squares** yellow.

Name _____

Identifying Rectangles

Color the **rectangles** red.

Reviewing Shapes

Trace the dotted lines to practice drawing each shape.

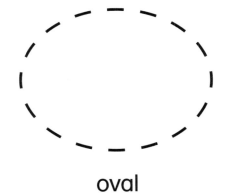

oval

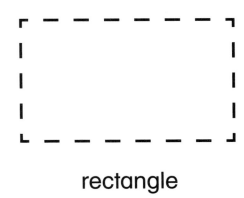

rectangle

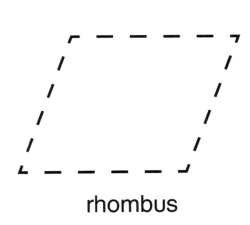

rhombus

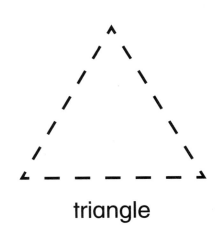

triangle

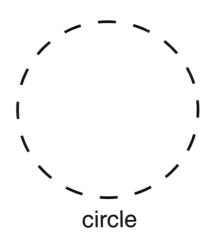

circle

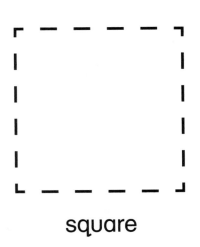

square

Name _____

Reviewing Shapes

Trace the dotted lines to complete the shapes.

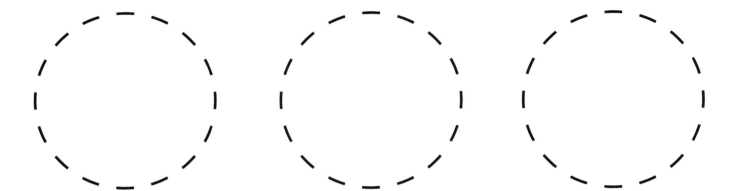

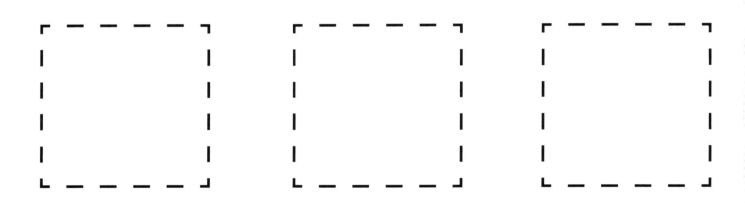

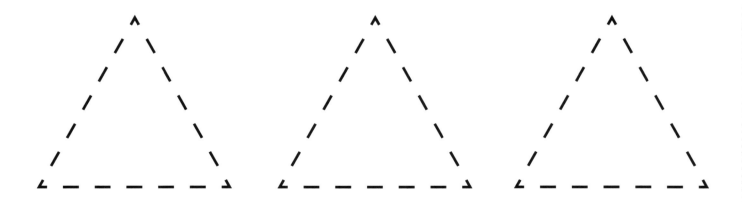

                    CD-104312 • © Carson-Dellosa

Name _____

Reviewing Shapes

Trace the dotted lines to complete the shapes.

Reviewing Shapes

Draw lines to match the shapes that are the **same**.
Color the matching shapes the same color.

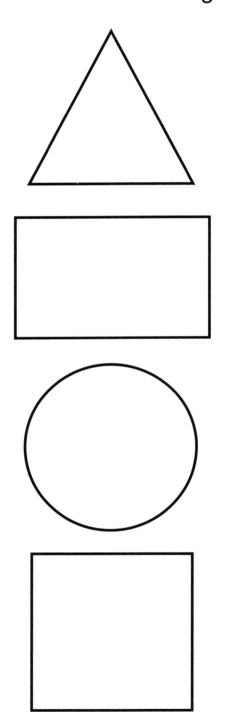

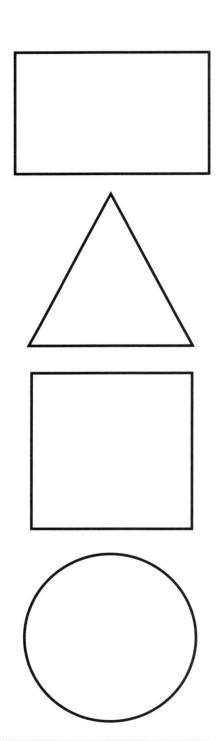

Name _____

Identifying Things That Do Not Belong

Circle the object that **does not** belong in each row.

Name _____

Identifying Things That Do Not Belong

Circle the object that **does not** belong in each row.

   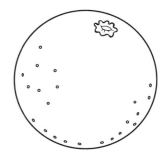

  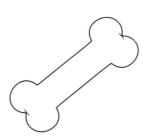 

   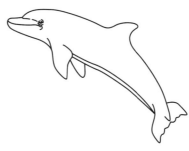

Identifying Things That Do Not Belong

Circle the object that **does not** belong in each row.

   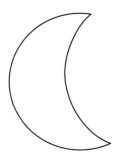

 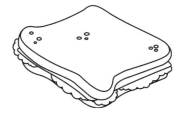  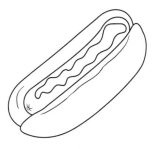

Name _____

Recognizing Things That Do Not Belong

Draw an X on the object that **does not** belong in each group.

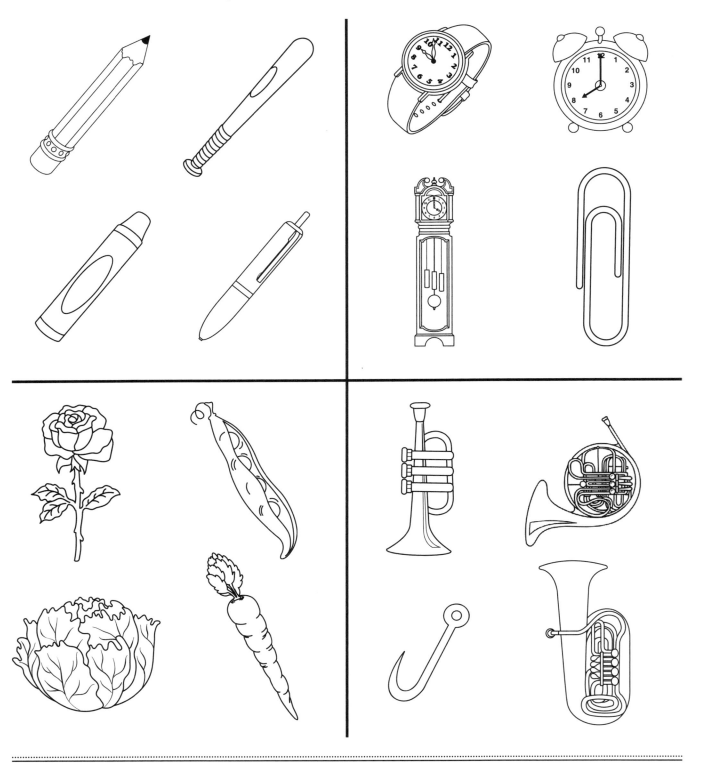

Name _____

Recognizing Things That Do Not Belong

Draw an X on the object that **does not** belong in each group.

Recognizing Things That Do Not Belong

Color the three objects that go together in each row.

Recognizing Things That Do Not Belong

Draw a line to match the two objects that go together in each group. Color the matching objects the same color.

Name _____

Recognizing Things That Do Not Belong

Draw lines to match the objects that go together. Color the matching objects the same color.

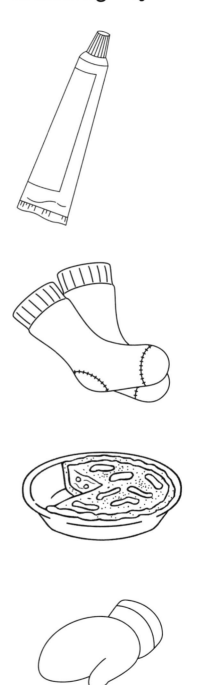

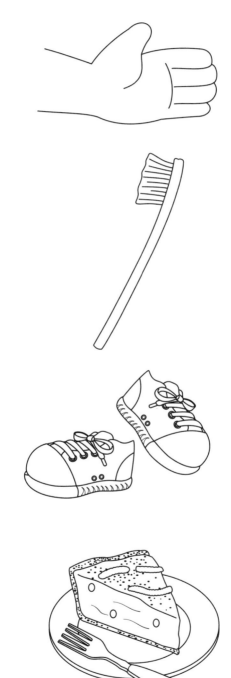

Name _____

Recognizing Things That Do Not Belong

Draw lines to match the objects that go together. Color the matching objects the same color.

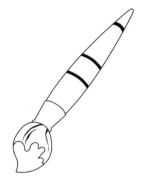

Name _____

Recognizing Things That Do Not Belong

Draw lines to match the objects that go together. Color the matching objects the same color.

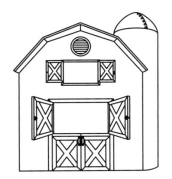

 CD-104312 • © Carson-Dellosa

Recognizing Rhyming Pairs

Draw lines to match the rhyming pairs. Color the pairs the same color.

mouse

bat

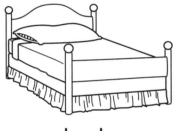

bed

log

cat

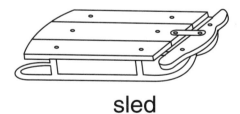

sled

frog

house

Recognizing Rhyming Pairs

Draw lines to match the rhyming pairs. Color the pairs the same color.

pail

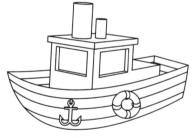

swing

dog

nail

ring

boat

goat

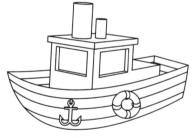

frog

Recognizing Rhyming Pairs

Draw lines to match the rhyming pairs. Color the pairs the same color.

book

jar

star

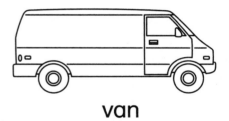

van

pan

mug

bug

hook

Name _____

Recognizing Rhyming Pairs

Circle the two objects that rhyme in each row.

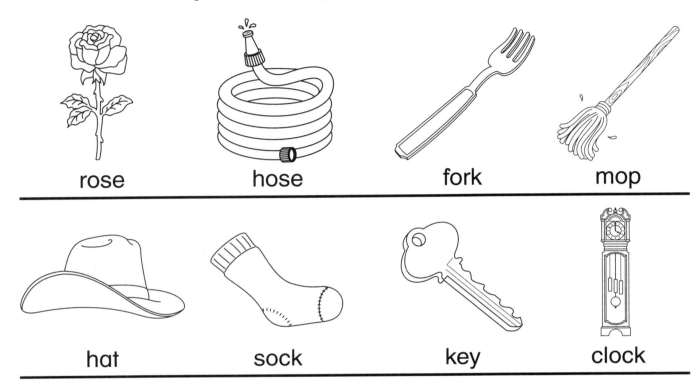

rose	hose	fork	mop

hat	sock	key	clock

eye	frog	fly	tree

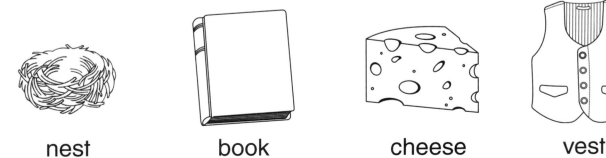

nest	book	cheese	vest

    CD-104312 • © Carson-Dellosa

Name _____

Recognizing Rhyming Pairs

Circle the two objects that rhyme in each row.

sock	cat	lock	ant

cow	boot	lamp	stamp

egg	leg	frog	pig

bus	key	bee	fish

Name _____

Recognizing What Comes Next

Complete each row by drawing the shape that comes **next** in the box.

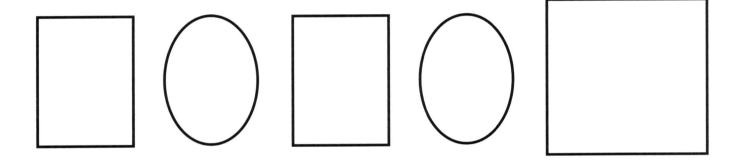

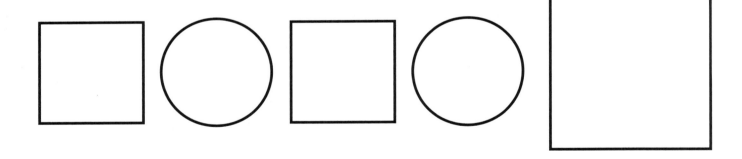

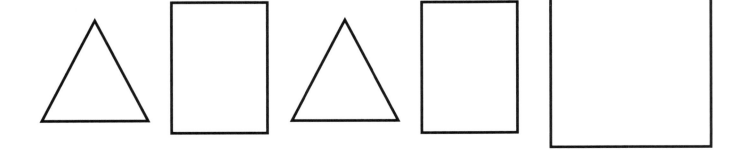

    CD-104312 • © Carson-Dellosa

Name _____

Recognizing What Comes Next

Finish each string of beads by completing the pattern.

Name _____

Recognizing What Comes Next

Complete each snake by drawing the shape that comes **next** in the pattern.

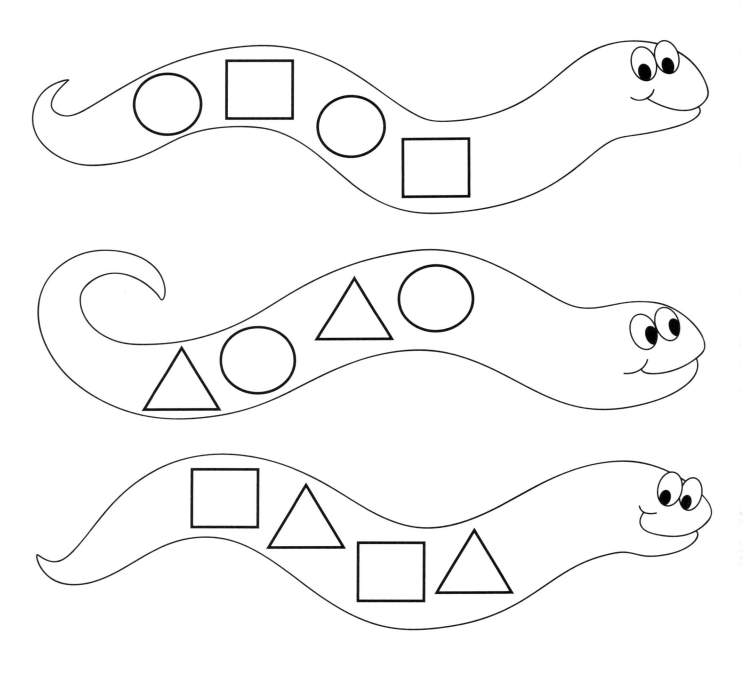

CD-104312 • © Carson-Dellosa

Name _____

Sequencing a Giraffe

Cut out the scrambled picture pieces.
Paste them together to make a giraffe
like the one on the right. Color the giraffe.

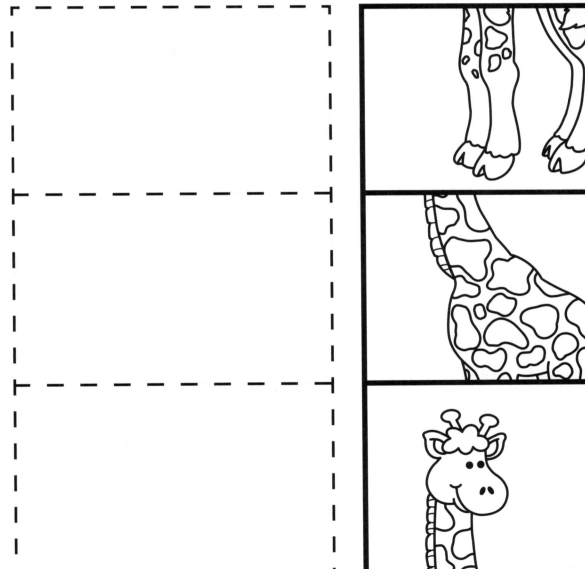

Name _____

Sequencing Grapes

Cut out the scrambled picture pieces.
Paste them together to make a bunch
of grapes like the one on the right.
Color the grapes.

CD-104312 • © Carson-Dellosa

Name _____

Sequencing a Tree

Cut out the scrambled picture pieces.
Paste them together to make a tree like
the one on the right. Color the tree.

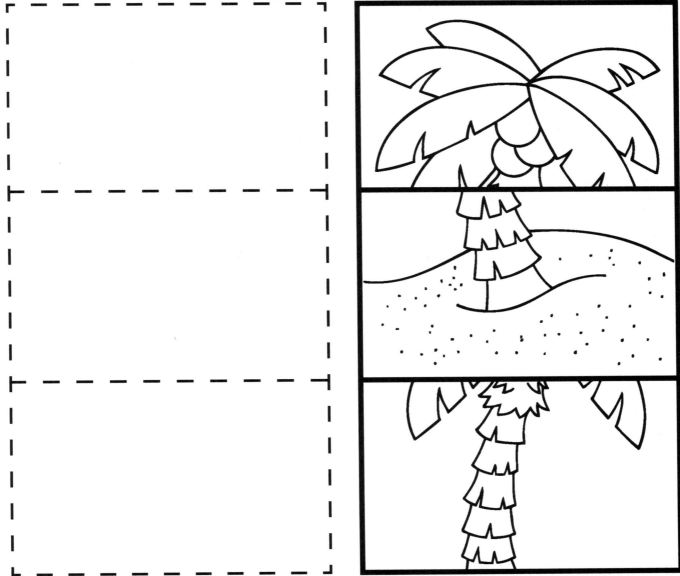

Name _____

Sequencing a Flamingo

Cut out the scrambled picture pieces.
Paste them together to make a flamingo
like the one on the right. Color the
flamingo.

 CD-104312 • © Carson-Dellosa

Name _____

Sequencing a Flower

Cut out the scrambled picture pieces.
Paste them together to make a flower
like the one on the right. Color the flower.

Name _____

Learning the Color Yellow

Use a **yellow** crayon to color the things that are usually **yellow**.

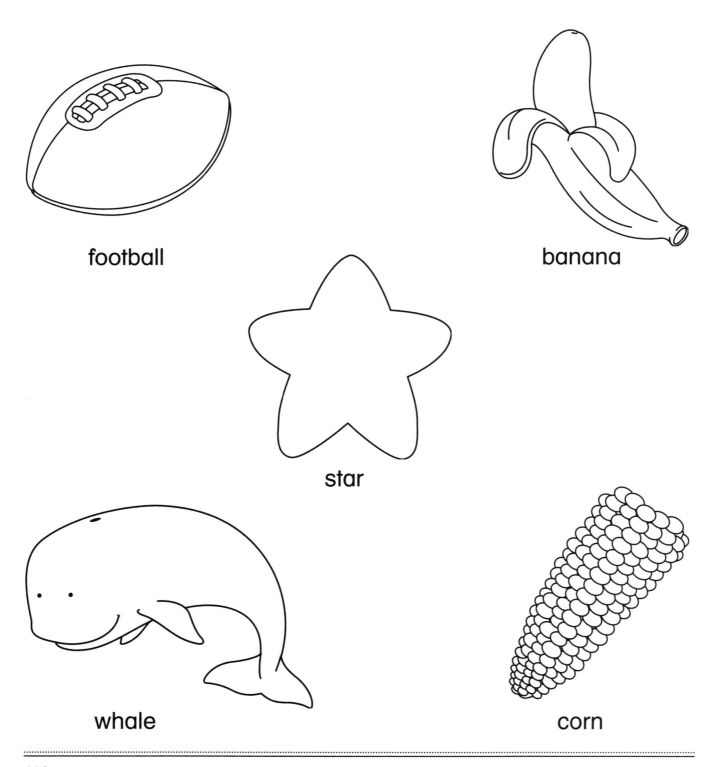

football

banana

star

whale

corn

Name _____

Learning the Color Green

Use a **green** crayon to color the things that are usually **green**.

frog

pig

lettuce

tree

sun

Name _____

Learning the Color Orange

Use an **orange** crayon to color the things that are usually **orange**.

apple

carrot

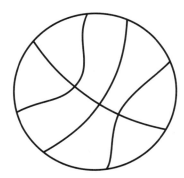

basketball

grapes

pumpkin

Name _____

Learning the Color Red

Use a **red** crayon to color the things that are usually **red**.

stop sign

strawberry

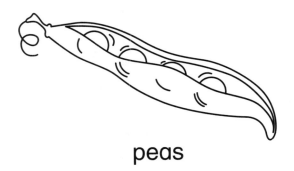

peas

nest

fire truck

Learning Colors

Color each picture the correct color.

orange carrot

red strawberry

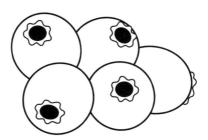

blue blueberries

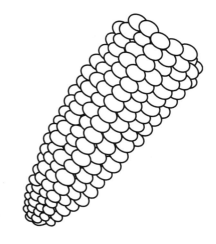

yellow corn

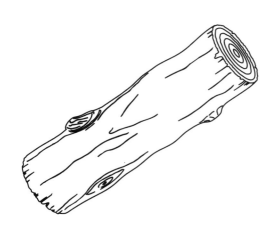

brown log

Name _____

Learning Colors

Color each picture the correct color.

gray whale

pink flower

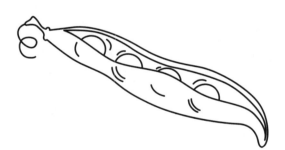

green peas

black bat

purple grapes

Name _____

Hidden Picture: Orange, Black, and Green

Color each space the correct color.

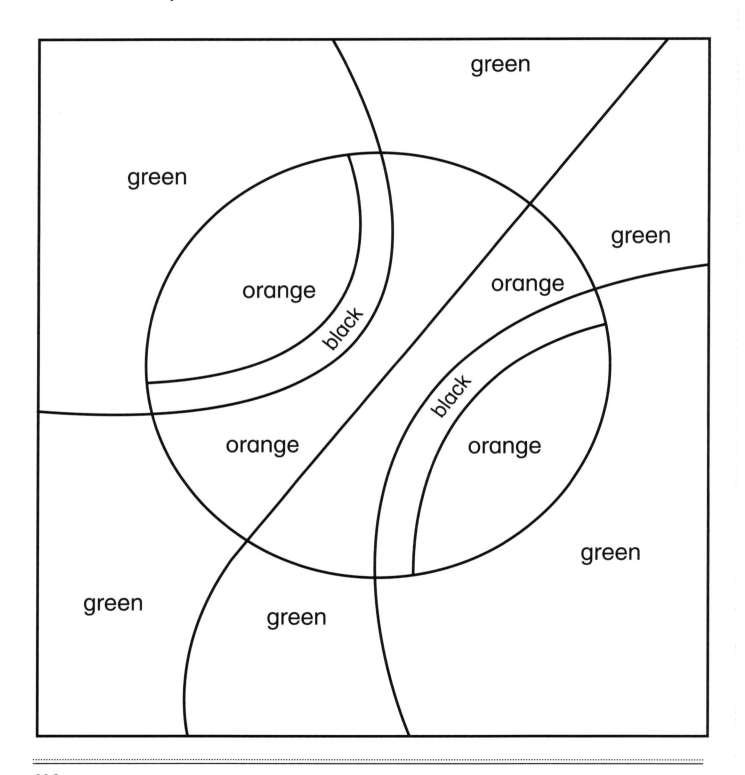

Name _____

Hidden Picture: Red, Green, and Pink

Color each space the correct color.

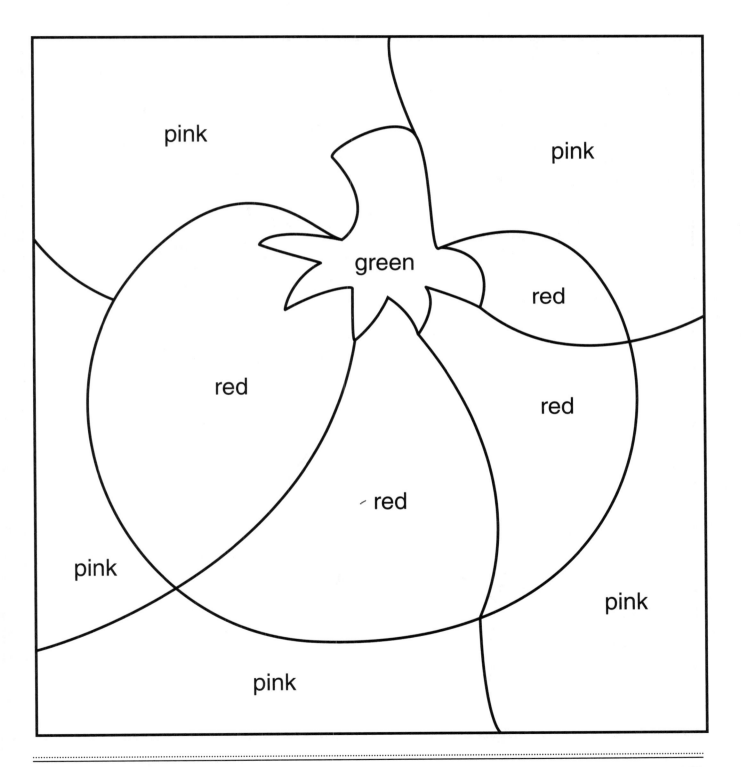

Name _____

Hidden Picture: Yellow and Blue

Color each space the correct color.

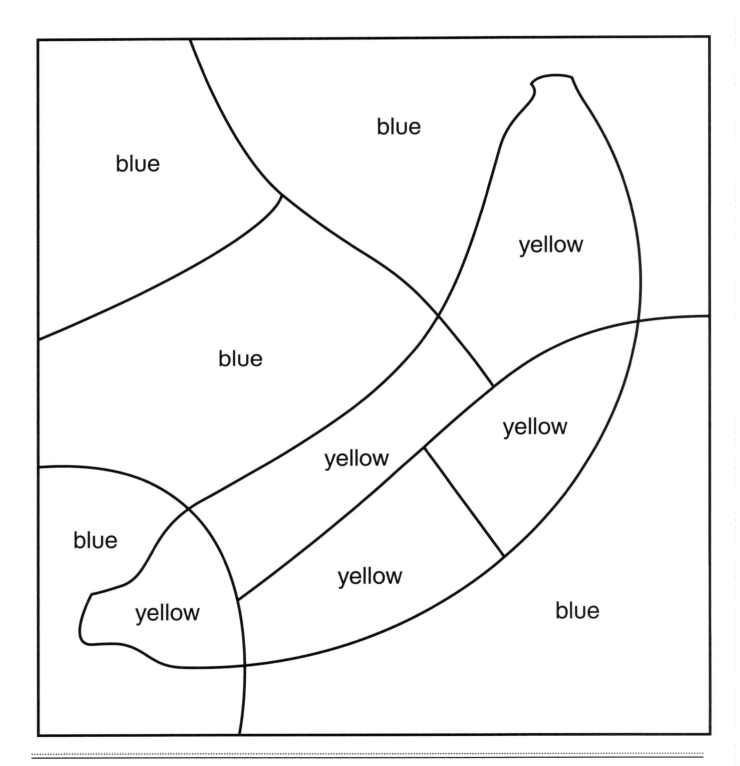

 CD-104312 • © Carson-Dellosa

Recognizing Colors

Color each balloon the correct color.

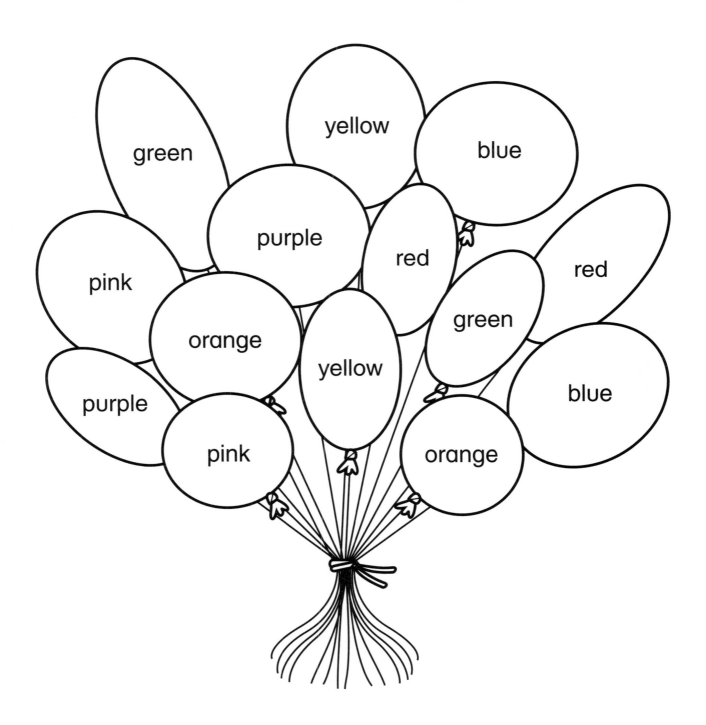

Counting 1–5

Draw a line to match each numeral to the correct amount of objects.

1

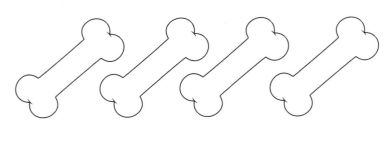

2

3

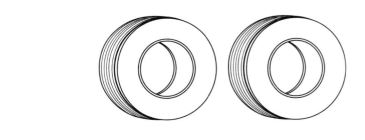

4

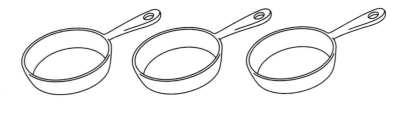

5

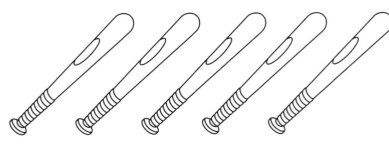

Counting 1–5

Draw a line to match each numeral to the correct amount of objects.

1

2

3

4

5

Counting 1–5

Color the correct number of objects in each row.

1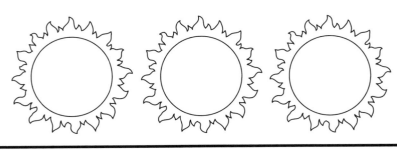

2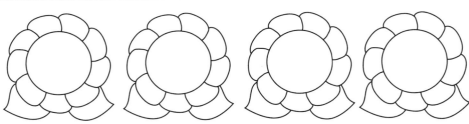

3

4

5

Name _____

Counting 6–10

Draw a line to match each numeral to the correct amount of objects.

6

7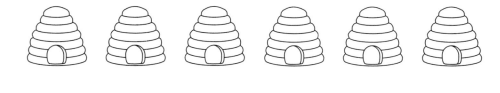

8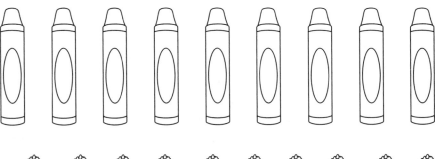

9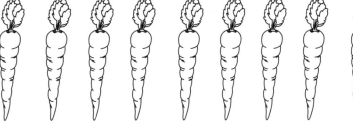

10

Counting 6–10

Color the correct number of objects in each row.

6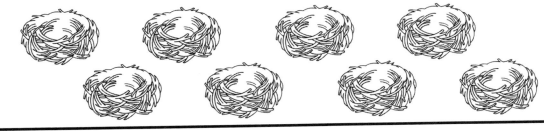

7

8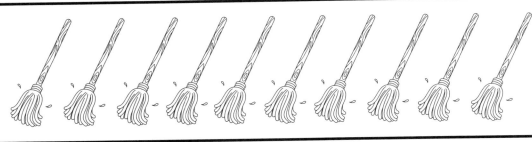

9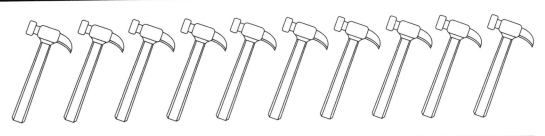

10

Counting 1–5

Trace each numeral. Draw a line to match each numeral to the correct number of leaves.

1
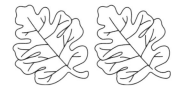

2

3

4

5

Counting 6–10

Trace each numeral. Draw a line to match each numeral to the correct number of leaves.

6

7

8

9

10

Name _____

Writing 0–4

• •

Practice writing each numeral.

0

1

2

3

4

Writing 5–9

Practice writing each numeral.

5

6

7

8

9

Congratulations!

_____

_____
receives this award for

_____

Date _____

Signed _____

three

seven

eleven

fifteen

two

six

ten

fourteen

one

five

nine

thirteen

zero

four

eight

twelve

sixteen	seventeen	eighteen	nineteen
twenty	twenty-one	twenty-two	twenty-three
twenty-four	twenty-five	twenty-six	twenty-seven
twenty-eight	twenty-nine	thirty	thirty-one

thirty-two	thirty-three	thirty-four	thirty-five
thirty-six	thirty-seven	thirty-eight	thirty-nine
forty	forty-one	forty-two	forty-three
forty-four	forty-five	forty-six	forty-seven

© CD

forty-eight   forty-nine   fifty   sixty

seventy   eighty   ninety   one hundred

+   −   =   >

>   a   b   c

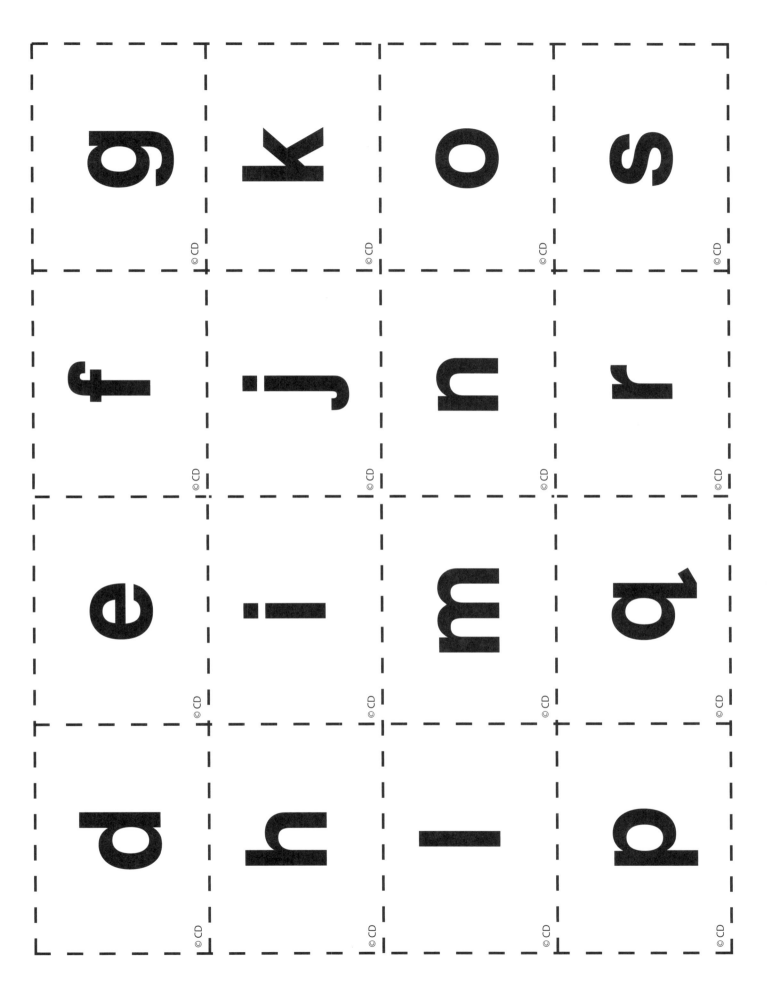

F   B   x   t

G   C   y   u

H   D   z   v

I   E   A   w

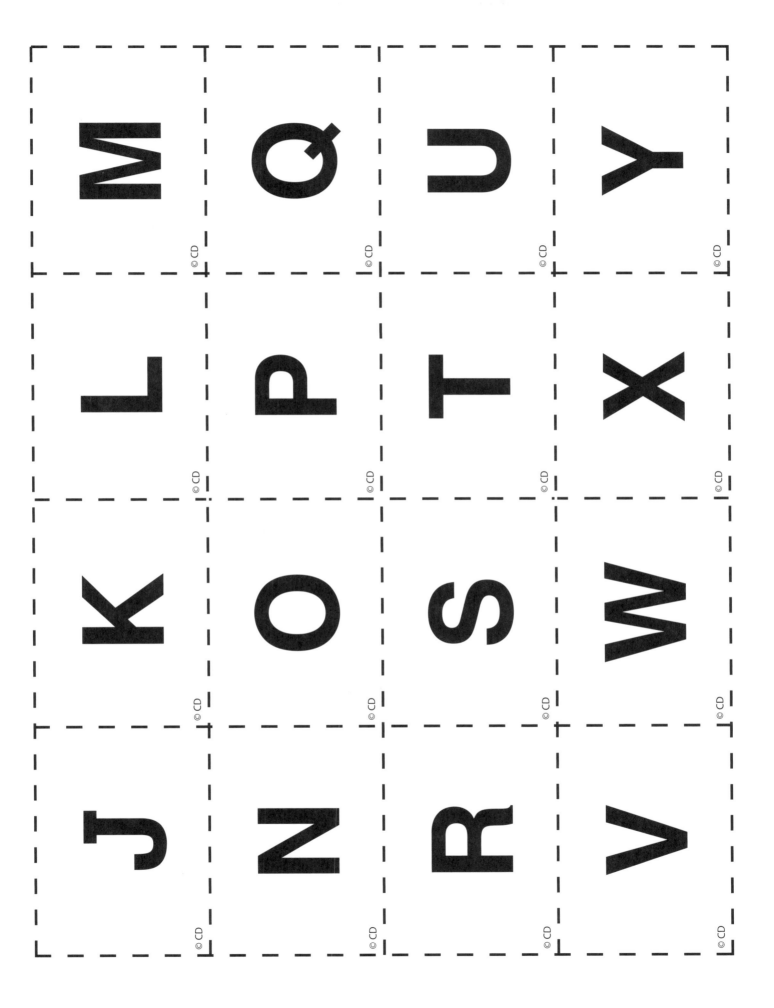

2 4 8 12

1 5 9 13

2 6 10 14

3 7 11 15

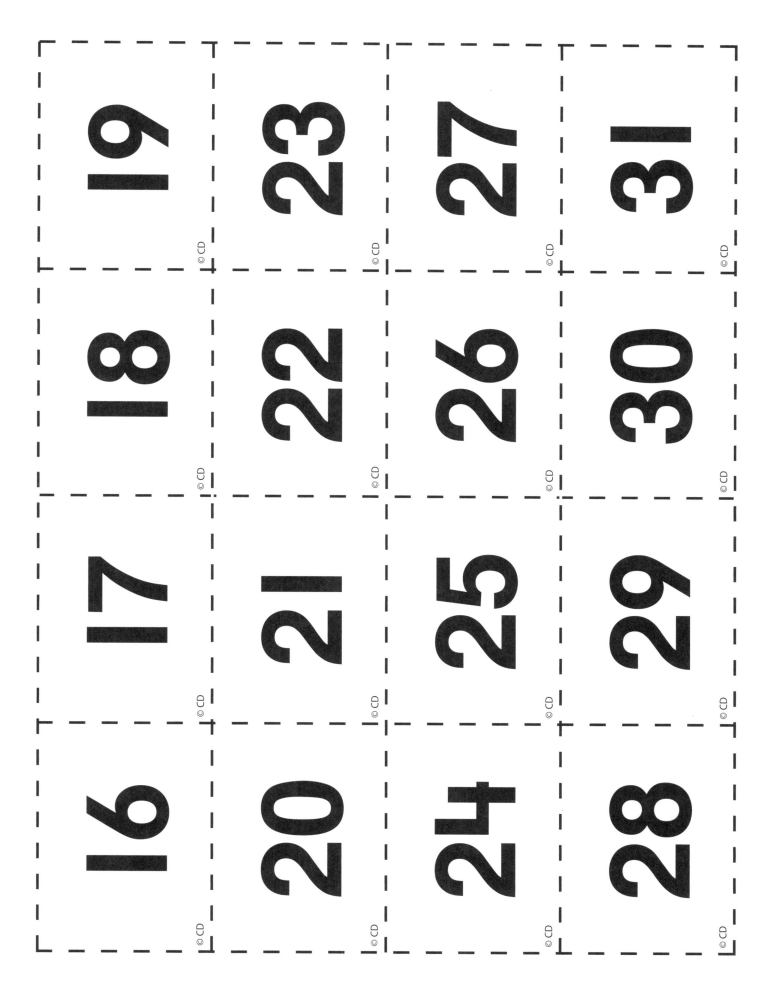

44	40	36	32
45	41	37	33
46	42	38	34
47	43	39	35

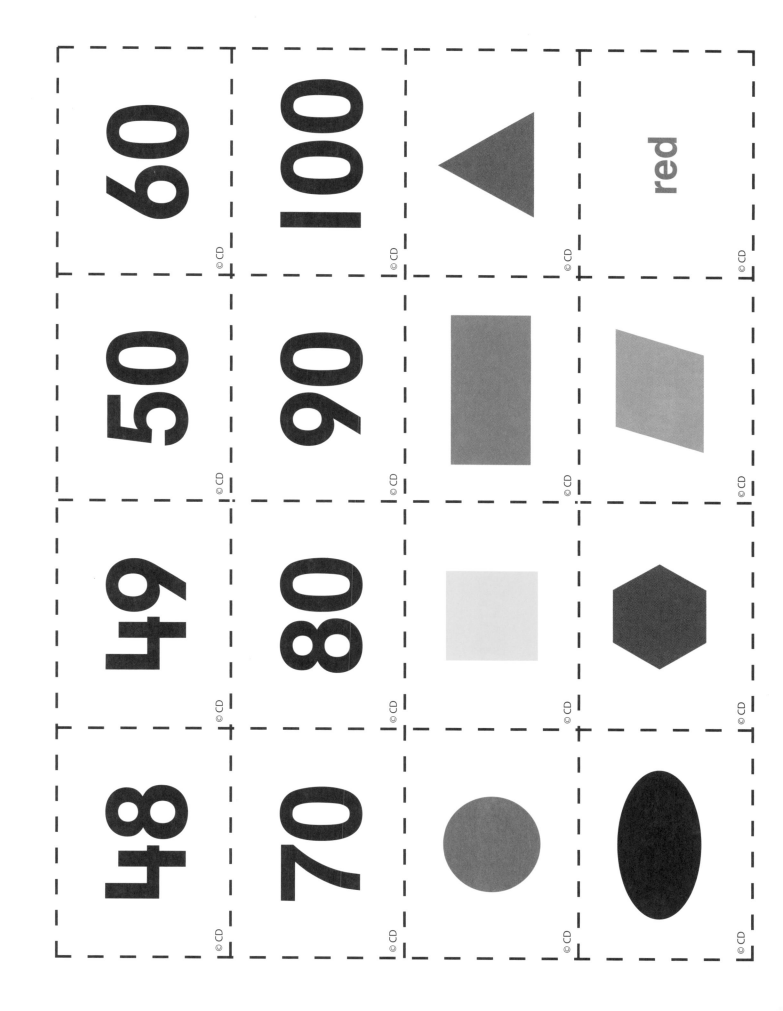

60

100

red

50

90

49

80

48

70

© CD

yellow

brown

triangle

green

orange

rectangle

rhombus

blue

square

hexagon

black

circle

oval